Provided
by

Measure B

which was approved by
the voters in
November, 1998

Games Around the World

Magic Tricks

by Cynthia Klingel and Robert B. Noyed

Content Adviser: Philip Willmarth, International Brotherhood of Magicians, Member of Inner Magic Circle
Social Science Adviser: Professor Sherry L. Field, Department of Curriculum and Instruction, College of Education, The University of Texas at Austin
Reading Adviser: Dr. Linda D. Labbo, Department of Reading Education, College of Education, The University of Georgia

COMPASS POINT BOOKS

MINNEAPOLIS, MINNESOTA

Compass Point Books
3109 West 50th Street, #115
Minneapolis, MN 55410

Visit Compass Point Books on the Internet at *www.compasspointbooks.com* or e-mail
your request to *custserv@compasspointbooks.com*

Photographs ©: Gregg Andersen, cover, 5, 27, 29; Wally McNamee/Corbis, 4;
Scala/Art Resource, N.Y., 6; Stock Montage, 7; North Wind Picture Archives, 8;
Bettmann/Corbis, 9; Kelly-Mooney Photography/Corbis, 10; Hulton Getty/Archive
Photos, 11, 14; Philip Gould/Corbis, 13.

Editors: E. Russell Primm and Emily J. Dolbear
Photo Researchers: Svetlana Zhurkina and Jo Miller
Photo Selector: Emily J. Dolbear
Designer: Bradfordesign, Inc.
Illustrator: Brandon Reibeling

Library of Congress Cataloging-in-Publication Data

Klingel, Cynthia Fitterer.
   Magic tricks / by Cynthia Klingel and Robert B. Noyed ; Content Adviser, Sherry L. Field;
Reading Adviser, Linda D. Labbo.
      p. cm. — (Games around the world)
   Includes bibliographical references and index.
   Summary: Presents a history of magic and magic tricks, along with tips and easy step-by-step
instructions for performing several tricks using coins and other common objects.
   ISBN 0-7565-0192-X (hardcover)
   1. Magic tricks—Juvenile literature. [1. Magic tricks.] I. Noyed, Robert B. II. Title. III. Series.
   GV1548 .K57 2002
   793.8—dc21   2001004744

Table of Contents

What Is a Magician? 5

The History of Magic 7

Magic Trick Basics 10

Falling Tower 16

Colorful Mind Reader 18

Mind Power! 20

Disappearing Quarter 22

Learning Magic Tricks 26

Glossary 28

Did You Know? 29

Want to Know More? 30

Index 32

What Is a Magician?

The **magician** on the stage wears a cape and a top hat. He is holding a **wand** in his hand. The magician seems to make flowers appear out of thin air. Then he produces a fluffy, white bunny from the empty top hat. He makes a red scarf turn green—right before your eyes!

Magicians make ordinary things act in surprising ways. They entertain and amaze people with their **magic tricks.**

You can become a magician by learning some simple tricks. It's not really magic, though—it just takes a lot of practice! So, are you ready to start learning some magic tricks?

▲ *A magician's wand*

◄ *A young magician performing a trick for family and friends*

The History of Magic

Magic is very old. Magic has been used for more than 4,000 years. People may have used magic to entertain people in ancient Egypt, Asia, and the Far East.

Priests in Greek temples used magic, too. In one magic trick, a voice came from a statue. Another trick started a fire in a vase. The priests called their tricks "the magic of the gods."

▲ A German woodcut of a sleight-of-hand trick

Early magic tricks used science. A magician would make a spark with static electricity. People believed that the magician had created fire.

Other early magic tricks focused on doing things the **audience** couldn't see. These are called **sleight-of-hand tricks.**

◀ A magician does a trick with cups and balls in this oil painting by Hiëronymus Bosch, who lived in the 1400s.

In the past, many people were afraid of magic. They thought it was the work of Satan, the devil. During the 1550s, people in Europe thought magic was the same as witch-craft. Many women were put to death

▲ *A woman is accused of being a witch.*

because people thought they were witches.

In time, people understood that magic was just tricks. Then they started seeing magic as entertainment.

In the mid-1800s, a French magician named Jean-Eugène Robert-Houdin made magic popular. He is one of the world's most famous magicians. He used science and clever tricks to amaze people.

Many other magicians began to travel around the world. One young magician in the United States called himself Harry Houdini, after Robert-Houdin. He became famous for escaping from handcuffs and jail cells.

Magic is still popular today. Children and adults around the world enjoy watching and performing magic tricks. Simple tricks use cups and balls, coins, and playing cards. Master magicians have used camels, goldfish, trains, and even the Statue of Liberty in their tricks!

▲ American magician Harry Houdini was famous for escaping from handcuffs.

Magic Trick Basics

All magicians follow certain rules. The most important rule is *never* to tell anyone how to do a trick. People always ask what the trick is, but the magician must never share the secret!

Another rule is very simple: Practice, practice, practice! A magician should be able to do the trick almost without thinking. If

▲ *Practice makes the tricks look easy.*

A magician lies on a bed of nails in 1955. ▶

you haven't practiced enough, you will make a mistake. Or worse, you will reveal the trick.

A third rule is: Try not to do the same magic trick for the same people. The more often someone sees your trick, the easier it is to figure the trick out.

An audience often wants to know what comes next in your trick. Don't tell them! Part of magic is surprising the audience. The element of surprise makes watching magic so much fun.

Magicians also do something called **patter.** Patter is the art of talking while you are doing a trick. The patter keeps the audience's attention. That makes it easier for the magician to do something without anyone seeing.

A street performer prepares to surprise his audience. ▶

Patter can also make a trick more interesting. A few moments of silence while you are setting up part of the trick helps build suspense. Just make sure your patter doesn't give the trick away.

Often magicians weave their tricks into a scary or funny story. They may use a **volunteer** from the audience to help them. Many magicians do a trick that contains many smaller tricks. The tricks are linked in ways that tell a larger tale.

◀ *A volunteer from the crowd helps a young magician do a trick in 1919.*

Falling Tower

In this trick, the magician pulls a piece of paper out from under a tower of coins without knocking the tower over.

What you need: A table, a capped soda bottle, a pile of quarters, and a strip of paper about 3 inches by 1½ inches (7.5 x 4 centimeters).

▲ *Make sure the paper hangs over on one side of the soda bottle.*

Setup:

1. Put the capped soda bottle on a table.

2. Place the paper on top of the bottle cap. Make sure one end of the paper hangs over on one side.

3. Pile the coins on top of the paper.

Trick:

1. Choose a volunteer from the audience. Ask him

or her to pull the paper out without knocking over the tower of coins. Most people will pull the paper slowly, and the tower will fall.

2. Set up the trick again.

3. Lick your forefinger. (Your forefinger is next to your thumb.) Then grasp the paper between your thumb and forefinger. Get a good hold!

4. Pull the paper out as quickly as you can. Make sure to bring your hand down, toward the table.

▲ *The trick is to pull down on the paper quickly.*

5. Raise your hand holding the paper in the air with a yell!

Colorful Mind Reader

In this trick, the magician claims to be a **mind reader** by naming the color of a crayon chosen by a volunteer.

What you need: Several crayons of different colors and a shoe box

Trick:

▲ *You'll need a shoe box and several crayons for this trick.*

1.   Choose a volunteer from the audience.

2.   Put your hands behind your back. Ask the volunteer to pick a crayon and put it in your hands without you seeing it.

3.   Ask the volunteer to put the other crayons in the shoe box and cover it.

4.   While the volunteer is busy, use your crayon to

secretly draw a mark on your thumbnail. Then put the crayon in your other hand.

5. Tell the volunteer that you must concentrate on the crayon together.

6. Place your fingertips on your forehead, pretending to concentrate. As you do this, look quickly to see the color on your thumbnail.

7. Announce that you know the answer. State the color dramatically!

8. Then bring the crayon from behind your back to show everyone. While the audience is looking at the crayon, carefully rub off the mark on your thumb with your forefinger.

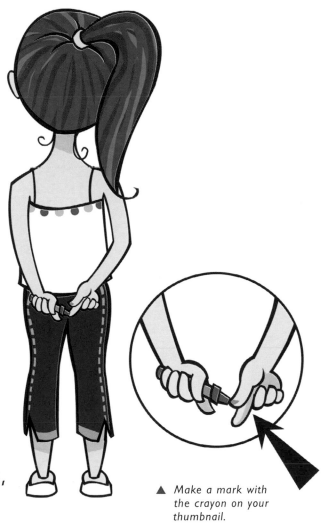

▲ Make a mark with the crayon on your thumbnail.

Mind Power!

In this trick, your assistant will read your mind. It requires teamwork.

What you need: A chair and an assistant

Trick:

1.   Introduce your assistant to the audience. Then ask your assistant to leave the room.

2.   Ask a volunteer from the audience to pick a number. You may want him or her to pick a number between one and ten.

▲ *Choose a volunteer.*

3.   Have your assistant return to the room.

4. Sit down in the chair. Then have the assistant stand behind you and put his or her fingers on the sides of your forehead to "receive" your thoughts.

5. When your assistant's fingers are on your temples, press your teeth together as many times as the chosen number.

6. After your assistant feels your temples moving under his or her fingers, have him or her announce the correct answer!

▲ *Have your assistant put his hands on your temples.*

21

Disappearing Quarter

Now you see it, now you don't! In this trick, the magician makes a quarter disappear. Remember, this trick takes some preparation and patience.

What you need: A quarter, three other coins, a small piece of aluminum foil, a pair of scissors, and a piece of cloth larger than your hand

Setup:

1. Place a small piece of aluminum foil over the quarter.

2. Press firmly against the foil and rub.

3. Continue until the foil has the features of the quarter rubbed onto it.

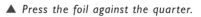
▲ *Press the foil against the quarter.*

4. Carefully lift the foil off the coin.

5. Use your scissors to cut around the edge of the foil coin.

6. Go slowly and be very careful! You do not want to bend the foil. You should end up with a piece of foil that looks just like a quarter.

7. Carefully place the foil onto the palm of your hand.

8. Put the other three coins around and over the edge of the foil. It should look like you have four coins in your hand.

▲ *Make sure the three coins overlap the foil quarter.*

Trick:

1. Hold out your hand to show your friends.

2. Ask them to remember the number of coins in your hand.

3. Place the cloth over the coins in your hand.

4. Close the hand holding the coins. You will start to fold the foil. Open and close your hand several times. You will fold and bend the foil into a wad. Your friends will hear only the coins jangling against one another.

5. Open your hand. The cloth is still covering the coins.

▲ *Close and open your hand under the cloth.*

24

6. With your other hand, grasp the cloth. Make sure you also grasp the wad of foil under the cloth.

7. Lift the cloth dramatically to show your open hand.

8. Drop the coins on a table for your friends to count.

9. While doing that, quietly let the ball of foil drop to the floor from under the cloth.

10. Then give your friends the cloth to examine. Where is the coin? It's magic!

▲ *Only three coins are left!*

Learning Magic Tricks

Some people like to learn magic tricks so they can put on a show. Others like to learn tricks so they can surprise and amaze their friends at work, at play, or at school. Whatever the reason, magic tricks are fun to learn and fun to perform.

You can learn many kinds of magic tricks. Some are easy and can be done with a few simple objects. Other tricks are more difficult. It takes a long time to learn the more difficult tricks.

The secret to doing magic tricks is practice. Now that you know how to do a few simple tricks, keep practicing them. You will soon be able to do these magic tricks very well. Then you'll be ready to become a real magician!

Two young magicians practice the Falling Tower trick! ▶

Glossary

audience—a group of people who listen to or watch a show

magician—someone who does magic tricks to entertain people

magic tricks—ways to make ordinary things act in surprising ways

mind reader—someone who claims to know another person's thoughts

patter—the art of talking during a magic trick to distract the audience

sleight-of-hand tricks—tricks that rely on doing things the audience can't see

volunteer—a helper from the audience

wand—a thin rod or stick used by magicians

Did You Know?

⭐ The fastest magician in the world is Eldon D. Wigton. In 1991, he performed 225 tricks in two minutes.

⭐ Harry Houdini died on Halloween night in 1926 in Detroit, Michigan.

⭐ The highest-paid magician in the world is David Copperfield. Copperfield's hometown is Metuchen, New Jersey.

⭐ Former boxer Muhammad Ali, Prince Charles, former U.S. president George H. W. Bush, and actor Steve Martin perform magic tricks as a hobby.

Want to Know More?

At the Library

Klutz Press, Ed. *Coin Magic.* Palo Alto, Calif.: Klutz, Inc., 1997.

Leyton, Lawrence. *My First Magic Book.* New York: Dorling Kindersley, 1993.

McMaster, Shawn, and Mike Moran. *Magic Tricks.* Los Angeles: Lowell House, 1999.

Setteducati, Mark, Anne Benkovitz, and Steve Ellis. *The Magic Show.* New York: Workman Publishing Company, 1999.

On the Web

For more information on *magic tricks,* use FactHound to track down Web sites related to this book.

1. Go to *http://www.compasspointbooks.com/facthound*
2. Type in this book ID: 075650192X
3. Click on the *Fetch It* button.

Your trusty FactHound will fetch the best Web sites for you!

Through the Mail

International Magicians Society

581 Ellison Avenue

Westbury, NY 11590

To get information about magic

On the Road

American Museum of Magic

107 East Michigan Avenue

Marshall, MI 49068

616/781-7666

To see an international collection of magic memorabilia

Index

acting, 12

audience, 12, 15

Colorful Mind Reader trick,
    18–19

Disappearing Quarter trick,
    22–25

escape tricks, 9

Falling Tower trick, 16–17

fire, 7

history of magic, 7–9

Houdini, Harry, 9

"magic of the gods," 7

magicians, 5

Mind Power trick, 20–21

patter, 12, 15

practice, 10, 12, 26

religion, 7, 8

Robert-Houdin, Jean-
    Eugène, 8–9

rules, 10, 12

science, 7, 9

sleight-of-hand tricks, 7

static electricity, 7

Statue of Liberty, 9

storytelling, 15

volunteers, 15

wands, 5

witchcraft, 8

About the Authors

Cynthia Klingel has worked as a high school English teacher and an elementary school teacher. She is currently the curriculum director for a Minnesota school district. Cynthia Klingel lives with her family in Mankato, Minnesota.

Robert B. Noyed started his career as a newspaper reporter. Since then, he has worked in school communications and public relations at the state and national level. Robert B. Noyed lives with his family in Brooklyn Center, Minnesota.